MORE
THINGS YOU CAN DO WITH A USELESS MAN

by
SCOTT WILSON

CCC PUBLICATIONS

Published by

CCC Publications
1111 Rancho Conejo Blvd.
Suites 411 & 412
Newbury Park, CA 91320

Published by arrangement with Reed Publishing (NZ) Ltd. of Auckland, New Zealand.
(First published by Reed Books of New Zealand ©1995 Scott Wilson)

U.S. version manufactured in the United States of America

Cover & interior art by Scott Wilson

Cover production by Oasis Graphics

ISBN: 0-918259-89-4

If your local U.S. bookstore is out of stock, copies of this book may be obtained by mailing check or money order for $5.95 per book (plus $2.50 to cover postage and handling) to: CCC Publications; 111 Rancho Conejo Blvd.; Suites 411 & 412; Newbury Park, CA 91320

Pre-publication Edition – 1/96

HANDY IN THE KITCHEN

MENDING THOSE LEAKY HOLES IN THE ROOF

STEP AEROBICS

SPARE TIRE

KEEPS THE FLIES OFF THE FOOD

QUICK TRIP TO THE MINI-MART

TOAST RACK

HAND TRUCK

ERASER

SHOE RACK

TIGER BATT

WASTEMASTER

RAKING THE YARD

POOPER SCOOPER

AAAACHOO!

STRIKE MASTER

NUTCRACKER

TV SWIVEL

WHERE'S THE LAST PLACE A
THIEF WOULD LOOK FOR YOUR JEWELLERY

ANCHOR

INTERIOR DECORATING

SHORTCUT THROUGH THE WOODS

YOU'LL FEEL BETTER AFTER YOU FRESHEN UP A LITTLE

BARSTOOL WITH ASHTRAY

BRAKE

BATTERING RAM

PENCIL SHARPENER

GREAT FOR HIKING

YOU CAN NEVER FIND ONE OF THOSE LITTLE BAGS WHEN YOU NEED ONE

APPLE CORER

CHEAP THRILLS

MOP UP THOSE MESSY SPILLS

SUNBLOCK

WINDSHIELD WIPER

MOUSETRAP

COMPACT DISC STORER

ICE FISHING MADE EASY

BALLAST

SORE HORSE

DOOR KNOCKER

SCAFFOLD

SUNDAY AFTERNOON IN THE PARK

WHO NEEDS A WOODEN DUMMY
WHEN YOU'VE GOT THE REAL THING

AUTOMATIC CLOTHES DRIER

BODY SURFING

THE ~~LEANING~~ TOWER OF PISA

HANDY FOR THOSE STUBBORN LIDS

TESTING THE NEW 'NIPPLE GUARD' BURGLAR ALARM

A GOOD WORKOUT

TITLES BY CCC PUBLICATIONS

Retail $4.99

"?"

POSITIVELY PREGNANT
SIGNS YOUR SEX LIFE IS DEAD
WHY MEN DON'T HAVE A CLUE
40 AND HOLDING YOUR OWN
CAN SEX IMPROVE YOUR GOLF?
THE COMPLETE BOOGER BOOK
THINGS YOU CAN DO WITH A USELESS MAN
FLYING FUNNIES
MARITAL BLISS & OXYMORONS
THE VERY VERY SEXY ADULT DOT-TO-DOT BOOK
THE DEFINITIVE FART BOOK
THE COMPLETE WIMP'S GUIDE TO SEX
THE CAT OWNER'S SHAPE UP MANUAL
PMS CRAZED: TOUCH ME AND I'LL KILL YOU!
RETIRED: LET THE GAMES BEGIN
MALE BASHING: WOMEN'S FAVORITE PASTIME
THE OFFICE FROM HELL
FOOD & SEX
FITNESS FANATICS
YOUNGER MEN ARE BETTER THAN RETIN-A
BUT OSSIFER, IT'S NOT MY FAULT

Retail $4.95

1001 WAYS TO PROCRASTINATE
THE WORLD'S GREATEST PUT-DOWN LINES
HORMONES FROM HELL II
SHARING THE ROAD WITH IDIOTS
THE GREATEST ANSWERING MACHINE
MESSAGES
    OF ALL TIME
WHAT DO WE DO NOW?? (A Guide For New
Parents)
HOW TO TALK YOU WAY OUT OF A TRAFFIC
TICKET
THE BOTTOM HALF (How To Spot Incompetent
    Professionals)
LIFE'S MOST EMBARRASSING MOMENTS
HOW TO ENTERTAIN PEOPLE YOU HATE
YOUR GUIDE TO CORPORATE SURVIVAL
THE SUPERIOR PERSON'S GUIDE TO EVERYDAY
    IRRITATIONS
GIFTING RIGHT

Retail $3.95
YOU KNOW YOU'RE AN OLD FART WHEN...
NO HANG-UPS
NO HANG-UPS II
NO HANG-UPS III
HOW TO SUCCEED IN SINGLES BARS
HOW TO GET EVEN WITH YOUR EXES
TOTALLY OUTRAGEOUS BUMPER-SNICKERS ($2.95)

Retail $5.95
MORE THINGS YOU CAN DO WITH A USELESS MAN
LITTLE INSTRUCTION BOOK OF THE RICH & FAMOUS
GETTING EVEN WITH THE ANSWERING MACHINE
ARE YOU A SPORTS NUT?
MEN ARE PIGS / WOMEN ARE BITCHES
50 WAYS TO HUSTLE YOUR FRIENDS ($5.99)
HORMONES FROM HELL
HUSBANDS FROM HELL
KILLER BRAS & Other Hazards Of The 50's
IT'S BETTER TO BE OVER THE HILL THAN UNDER IT
HOW TO REALLY PARTY!!!
WORK SUCKS!
THE PEOPLE WATCHER'S FIRLD GUIDE
THE UNOFFICIAL WOMEN'S DIVORCE GUIDE

Retail $5.95 (continued)
THE ABSOLUTE LAST CHANCE DIET BOOK
FOR MEN ONLY (How To Survive Marriage)
THE UGLY TRUTH ABOUT MEN
NEVER A DULL CARD
RED HOT MONOGAMY
   (In Just 60 Seconds A Day) ($6.95)

NO HANG-UPS – CASSETTES Retail $4.98
Vol. I: GENERAL MESSAGES (Female)
Vol. I: GENERAL MESSAGES (Male)
Vol. II: BUSINESS MESSAGES (Female)
Vol. II: BUSINESS MESSAGES (Male)
Vol. III: 'R' RATED MESSAGES (Female)
Vol. III: 'R' RATED MESSAGES (Male)
Vol. IV: SOUND EFFECTS ONLY
Vol. V: CELEBRI-TEASE